AF386885

LION
CHILDREN'S

In the little town of Nazareth lived a young woman named Mary. She was looking forward to getting married.

One day, an angel came to visit her.

"Don't be afraid," said the angel.

"God has chosen
you for something
very special. You are
going to have a baby:
God's own Son. You
must call him Jesus. He
will bring God's blessings to the world."

Mary was very surprised but she
agreed. "I will do as God
wants," she said.

Mary was looking forward to
marrying Joseph. But when
Joseph heard Mary's news,
he was worried.

Then an angel spoke to
him in a dream. "Take
care of Mary," said
the angel. "Her baby
is God's own Son.
He will bring God's
blessings to all the world."

Joseph was very puzzled, but he said he
would take care of Mary.

And together they went to
take part in a great counting
of people that was being done.
They went to Bethlehem.

The town was very
busy. The only place
to stay was in a room
full of animals.

There, Mary's baby was born. Mary
wrapped him in swaddling clothes.
She laid him to sleep in a manger.

Out in the fields nearby,
shepherds were watching
their sheep. An angel appeared.

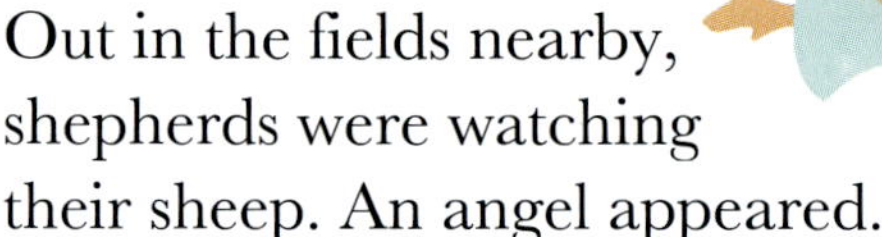

"Do not be afraid," said the angel.
"Tonight, in Bethlehem, a baby
has been born: God's special
king, who will bring
God's blessings to
the world."

Then all the angels sang
together for joy.

The shepherds went to Bethlehem.

They found Mary and the baby,
just as the angel had said.

Far away, wise men saw a special
star in the night sky.

"It is a sign that a new king has
been born," they said. "We must
go and find him."

The star led them to the place
where Jesus was.

They brought him gifts: gold,
frankincense and myrrh.

Mary smiled. The gifts for Jesus were gifts for a king.

"The king who will bring God's blessings to the world," she said to herself.

Special Words

angel	a messenger from God
blessing	a good gift from God
frankincense	amber nuggets that make a fire smell sweet
gold	a precious metal
manger	a feeding box for animals
myrrh	pink ointment
shepherd	someone who looks after sheep
swaddling	wrap-around baby clothes

A Prayer

Bless me at Christmas time,
and all through the year.

Bless those I love at Christmas time,
and all through the year.

Bless everyone at Christmas time,
and all through the year.

Text by Lois Rock
Illustrations copyright © 2003 Alex Ayliffe
This edition copyright © 2011 Lion Hudson IP Limited

Published by
Lion Children's Books
www.lionhudson.com
Part of the SPCK Group
SPCK, Studio 101, The Record Hall, 16–16A Baldwin's Gardens, London EC1N 7RJ

ISBN 978 0 7459 6310 5
e-ISBN 978 0 7459 6744 8

First edition 2005
This edition 2011

A catalogue record for this book is available from the British Library

Printed and bound in China, June 2025, LH54